ELECTRIFY AFRICA ACT OF 2013

MARKUP

BEFORE THE

COMMITTEE ON FOREIGN AFFAIRS
HOUSE OF REPRESENTATIVES

ONE HUNDRED THIRTEENTH CONGRESS

SECOND SESSION

ON

H.R. 2548

FEBRUARY 27, 2014

Serial No. 113–117

Printed for the use of the Committee on Foreign Affairs

Available via the World Wide Web: http://www.foreignaffairs.house.gov/ or
http://www.gpo.gov/fdsys/

U.S. GOVERNMENT PRINTING OFFICE

86–871PDF   WASHINGTON : 2014

For sale by the Superintendent of Documents, U.S. Government Printing Office
Internet: bookstore.gpo.gov   Phone: toll free (866) 512–1800; DC area (202) 512–1800
Fax: (202) 512–2104   Mail: Stop IDCC, Washington, DC 20402–0001

COMMITTEE ON FOREIGN AFFAIRS

EDWARD R. ROYCE, California, *Chairman*

CHRISTOPHER H. SMITH, New Jersey
ILEANA ROS-LEHTINEN, Florida
DANA ROHRABACHER, California
STEVE CHABOT, Ohio
JOE WILSON, South Carolina
MICHAEL T. McCAUL, Texas
TED POE, Texas
MATT SALMON, Arizona
TOM MARINO, Pennsylvania
JEFF DUNCAN, South Carolina
ADAM KINZINGER, Illinois
MO BROOKS, Alabama
TOM COTTON, Arkansas
PAUL COOK, California
GEORGE HOLDING, North Carolina
RANDY K. WEBER SR., Texas
SCOTT PERRY, Pennsylvania
STEVE STOCKMAN, Texas
RON DeSANTIS, Florida
DOUG COLLINS, Georgia
MARK MEADOWS, North Carolina
TED S. YOHO, Florida
LUKE MESSER, Indiana

ELIOT L. ENGEL, New York
ENI F.H. FALEOMAVAEGA, American Samoa
BRAD SHERMAN, California
GREGORY W. MEEKS, New York
ALBIO SIRES, New Jersey
GERALD E. CONNOLLY, Virginia
THEODORE E. DEUTCH, Florida
BRIAN HIGGINS, New York
KAREN BASS, California
WILLIAM KEATING, Massachusetts
DAVID CICILLINE, Rhode Island
ALAN GRAYSON, Florida
JUAN VARGAS, California
BRADLEY S. SCHNEIDER, Illinois
JOSEPH P. KENNEDY III, Massachusetts
AMI BERA, California
ALAN S. LOWENTHAL, California
GRACE MENG, New York
LOIS FRANKEL, Florida
TULSI GABBARD, Hawaii
JOAQUIN CASTRO, Texas

AMY PORTER, *Chief of Staff*   THOMAS SHEEHY, *Staff Director*
JASON STEINBAUM, *Democratic Staff Director*

CONTENTS

ELECTRIFY AFRICA ACT OF 2013

THURSDAY, FEBRUARY 27, 2014

House of Representatives,
Committee on Foreign Affairs,
Washington, DC.

The committee met, pursuant to notice, at 10:06 a.m., in room 2172 Rayburn House Office Building, Hon. Edward Royce (chairman of the committee) presiding.

Chairman ROYCE. The committee will come to order. I will ask members to take their seats. And pursuant to notice, we need today to mark up H.R. 2548, the Electrify Africa Act. And without objection, all members may have 5 legislative days to submit statements for the record or any extraneous materials for today's bill. So I will now call up H.R. 2548. Without objection, the bill is considered read.

The Royce-Engel amendment in the nature of a substitute that was provided to your offices Tuesday morning is considered base text for purposes of the markup and is open for amendment at any point. And after my brief remarks, I will recognize the ranking member, Mr. Engel from New York, and then any other members seeking recognition to speak on today's bill.

[The information referred to follows:]

113TH CONGRESS
1ST SESSION

H. R. 2548

To establish a comprehensive United States Government policy to assist countries in sub-Saharan Africa to develop an appropriate mix of power solutions for more broadly distributed electricity access in order to support poverty alleviation and drive economic growth, and for other purposes.

IN THE HOUSE OF REPRESENTATIVES

JUNE 27, 2013

Mr. ROYCE (for himself, Mr. ENGEL, Mr. SMITH of New Jersey, and Ms. BASS) introduced the following bill; which was referred to the Committee on Foreign Affairs, and in addition to the Committee on Financial Services, for a period to be subsequently determined by the Speaker, in each case for consideration of such provisions as fall within the jurisdiction of the committee concerned

---

A BILL

To establish a comprehensive United States Government policy to assist countries in sub-Saharan Africa to develop an appropriate mix of power solutions for more broadly distributed electricity access in order to support poverty alleviation and drive economic growth, and for other purposes.

1   *Be it enacted by the Senate and House of Representa-*

2 *tives of the United States of America in Congress assembled,*

1 **SECTION 1. SHORT TITLE.**

2   This Act may be cited as the "Electrify Africa Act

3 of 2013".

4 **SEC. 2. PURPOSE.**

5   The purpose of this Act is to improve access to af-

6 fordable, reliable electricity in Africa in order to unlock

7 the potential for economic growth, job creation, food secu-

8 rity, improved health and education outcomes, and sus-

9 tainable poverty reduction.

10 **SEC. 3. FINDINGS.**

11   Congress finds that—

12   (1) 589,000,000 people in sub-Saharan Africa,

13   or 68 percent of the population, do not have access

14   to electricity, as of 2010;

15   (2) electricity services are highly unreliable and

16   remain at least twice as expensive compared to other

17   emerging regions for the majority of people with ac-

18   cess to electricity in sub-Saharan Africa;

19   (3) lack of access to electricity services dispro-

20   portionally affects women—who often shoulder the

21   burden of seeking sources of heat and light such as

22   dung, wood or charcoal and are often more exposed

23   to the associated negative health impacts. Women

24   and girls also face increase risks of assault from

25   walking long distances to gather fuel sources;

1 (4) people without access to electricity are often

2 trapped in subsistence lifestyles and are unable to

3 work their way out of poverty;

4 (5) a lack of electricity contributes to the high

5 use of inefficient and often highly polluting fuel

6 sources for indoor cooking, heating, and lighting

7 that produce toxic fumes resulting in more than

8 3,000,000 annual premature deaths from respiratory

9 disease, more annual deaths than from HIV/AIDS

10 and malaria in sub-Saharan Africa;

11 (6) electricity access is crucial for the storage

12 of vaccines and anti-retroviral and other lifesaving

13 medical drugs, as well as the operation of modern

14 lifesaving medical equipment;

15 (7) electricity access can be used to improve

16 food security by enabling post-harvest processing,

17 pumping, irrigation, dry grain storage, milling, re-

18 frigeration, and other uses;

19 (8) electricity access can provide improved

20 lighting options, internet access, mobile phone

21 charging, and other new information and commu-

22 nication technologies that can greatly improve health

23 and education outcomes as well as commercial possi-

24 bilities;

1   (9) Africa's consumer base of 1,000,000,000

2   people is rapidly growing and will create increasing

3   demand for United States goods, services, and tech-

4   nologies, but the current African electricity deficit

5   limits this growth in demand by restricting economic

6   growth on the continent;

7   (10) approximately 30 African countries face

8   endemic power shortages, and nearly 70 percent of

9   surveyed African businesses cite unreliable power as

10 a major constraint to growth;

11   (11) the Millennium Challenge Corporation's

12 work in the energy sector shows high projected eco-

13 nomic rates of returns that translate to sustainable

14 economic growth and that the highest returns are

15 projected when infrastructure improvements are cou-

16 pled with significant legislative and regulatory and

17 institutional policy reforms;

18   (12) in some countries, regulatory bottlenecks

19 and legal constraints stifle the ability of private in-

20 vestment to assist in the generation and distribution

21 of electricity; and

22   (13) without new policies and more effective in-

23 vestments in electricity sector enterprises to increase

24 and expand electricity access in sub-Saharan Africa,

25 over 70 percent of the rural population, and 48 per-

1 cent of the total population, will remain without ac-
2 cess to electricity by 2030.

3 **SEC. 4. STATEMENT OF POLICY.**

4 Congress declares that it is the policy of the United
5 States, in consultation with sub-Saharan African govern-
6 ments, to—

7 (1) encourage the installation of at least an ad-
8 ditional 20,000 megawatts of electrical power in sub-
9 Saharan Africa by 2020;

10 (2) promote first-time access to electricity for
11 at least 50,000,000 people in sub-Saharan Africa by
12 2020 in both urban and rural areas; and

13 (3) promote efficient institutional platforms to
14 provide electrical service to rural and underserved
15 areas.

16 **SEC. 5. DEVELOPMENT OF A COMPREHENSIVE, MULTIYEAR**
17 **STRATEGY.**

18 (a) STRATEGY.—The President shall establish a com-
19 prehensive, integrated, multiyear strategy to assist coun-
20 tries in sub-Saharan Africa to develop an appropriate mix
21 of power solutions, including renewable energy, to provide
22 sufficient electricity access to people living in rural and
23 urban areas in order to alleviate poverty and drive eco-
24 nomic growth. Such strategy shall maintain sufficient

1 flexibility and remain responsive to technological innova-

2 tion in the power sector.

3   (b) REPORT.—

4   (1) IN GENERAL.—Not later than 180 days

5   after the date of the enactment of this Act, the

6   President shall transmit to the appropriate congres-

7   sional committees a report setting forth the strategy

8   described in subsection (a).

9   (2) REPORT CONTENTS.—The report required

10   by paragraph (1) shall include a discussion of the

11   elements described in paragraph (3), and should in-

12   clude a discussion of any additional elements rel-

13   evant to the strategy described in subsection (a).

14   (3) REPORT ELEMENTS.—The elements re-

15   ferred to in paragraph (2) are the following:

16   (A) The general and specific objectives of

17   the strategy described in subsection (a), the cri-

18   teria for determining success of the strategy,

19   and a description of the manner in which the

20   strategy will increase production and improve

21   access to electricity.

22   (B) Development of plans and regulations

23   at the national, regional, and local level to in-

24   crease power production, strengthen electrical

1   transmission and distribution infrastructure,

2   and improve access to electricity.

3   (C) Administration plans to increase access

4   to electricity, including a description of how the

5   strategy will address commercial and residential

6   needs, as well as urban and rural access.

7   (D) Administration strategy to reduce

8   waste and improve existing power generation

9   through the use of a broad power mix and use

10   of a distributed generation model.

11   (E) Administration policy on engaging and

12   leveraging private sector resources and public

13   sector financing.

14   (F) A description of the strategy for the

15   transfer of relevant technology and skills to

16   local participation in the long-term maintenance

17   and management of such investments to ensure

18   power sector investments are sustainable, in-

19   cluding the details of the programs to be under-

20   taken to maximize United States contributions

21   in the areas of technical assistance and train-

22   ing.

23   (G) An identification of the relevant execu-

24   tive branch agencies that will be involved in car-

25   rying out the strategy, the level and distribution

1 of resources that will be dedicated on an annual

2 basis among the such agencies, the assignment

3 of priorities to such agencies, a description of

4 the role of each agency, and the types of pro-

5 grams that each agency will be undertaking.

6 (H) A description of the mechanisms that

7 will be utilized to coordinate the efforts of the

8 relevant executive branch agencies in carrying

9 out the strategy to avoid duplication of efforts,

10 enhance coordination, and ensure that each

11 agency undertakes programs primarily in those

12 areas where each such agency has the greatest

13 expertise, technical capabilities, and potential

14 for success.

15 (I) A description of the mechanisms to be

16 established for monitoring and evaluating in-

17 creased electricity access development, for

18 learning and transmitting best practices among

19 relevant executive branch agencies as well as

20 among participating countries, and for termi-

21 nating unsuccessful programs.

22 (J) A description of the engagement plan

23 for working with local communities benefitting

24 from the projects and affected by the projects

1   as well as the environment and social impacts

2   of the projects.

3   (K) A description of the mechanisms that

4   will be utilized to ensure greater coordination

5   between the United States and foreign govern-

6   ments, international organizations, African re-

7   gional economic communities, international fi-

8   nancial institutions, and private sector organi-

9   zations.

10   (L) A description of how United States

11   leadership will be used to enhance the overall

12   international response to prioritizing electricity

13   access for sub-Saharan Africa and to strength-

14   en coordination among relevant international

15   forums such as the G8 and G20.

16   (M) An outline of how the Administration

17   intends to partner with foreign governments,

18   the World Bank Group, the African Develop-

19   ment Bank Group, and the public sector to as-

20   sist sub-Saharan African countries to conduct

21   project feasibility studies and facilitate project

22   development.

23   (N) A description of how the Administra-

24   tion intends to help facilitate transnational and

1   regional power and electrification projects

2   where appropriate.

3 **SEC. 6. USAID.**

4   (a) LOAN GUARANTEES.—It is the sense of Congress

5 that in pursuing the policy goals described in section 4,

6 the Administrator of USAID should identify and

7 prioritize—

8   (1) where loan guarantees to local African fi-

9   nancial institutions would facilitate the involvement

10   of such financial institutions in power projects in Af-

11   rica; and

12   (2) where partnerships and grants for research,

13   development, and deployment of technology would

14   increase access to electricity in Africa.

15   (b) GRANTS.—It is the sense of Congress that the

16 Administrator of USAID, acting through USAID's Bu-

17 reau for Africa and Economic Growth, Education and En-

18 vironment, should consider providing grants to—

19   (1) develop national, regional, and local energy

20   and electricity policy plans;

21   (2) expand distribution of electricity access to

22   the poorest; and

23   (3) build a country's capacity to monitor and

24   regulate the energy and electricity sector.

1   (c) USAID DEFINED.—In this section, the term

2 "USAID" means the United States Agency for Inter-

3 national Development.

4 **SEC. 7. DEPARTMENT OF THE TREASURY.**

5   In pursuing the policy goals described in section 4,

6 the Secretary of the Treasury should direct the United

7 States Executive Director at each institution in the World

8 Bank Group and the African Development Bank to use

9 the voice, vote, and influence of the United States to en-

10 courage each such entity to—

11   (1) commit to significantly increase power sec-

12   tor and electrification investments in sub-Saharan

13   Africa;

14   (2) consider energy needs of individuals where

15   access to an electricity grid is impractical or cost-

16   prohibitive;

17   (3) enhance coordination with the private sector

18   in sub-Saharan Africa to increase access to elec-

19   tricity;

20   (4) provide technical assistance to the regu-

21   latory authorities of sub-Saharan African govern-

22   ments to remove unnecessary barriers to investment

23   in commercially viable projects, reduce transmission

24   and distribution losses, encourage end-use efficiency,

1   strengthen local markets, and unlock domestic in-

2   vestment in the power sector; and

3   (5) utilize clear, accountable, and metric-based

4   targets to measure the effectiveness of such projects.

5 **SEC. 8. OVERSEAS PRIVATE INVESTMENT CORPORATION.**

6   (a) IN GENERAL.—The Overseas Private Investment

7 Corporation should—

8   (1) in carrying out its programs and pursuing

9   the policy goals described in section 4, place a pri-

10   ority on supporting investment in the electricity sec-

11   tor of sub-Saharan Africa and implement procedures

12   for expedited review of and, where appropriate, ap-

13   proval of, applications by eligible investors for loans,

14   loan guarantees, and insurance for such investments;

15   (2) to the extent permitted by its authorities,

16   policies, and programs, support investments in

17   projects that will—

18   (A) maximize the number of people with

19   new access to electricity to support economic

20   development;

21   (B) improve the transmission and distribu-

22   tion of electricity;

23   (C) provide reliable and low-cost electricity

24   to people living in rural and urban commu-

25   nities;

1   (D) consider energy needs of individuals

2   where access to an electricity grid is impractical

3   or cost-prohibitive; and

4   (E) reduce transmission and distribution

5   losses and improve end-use efficiency;

6   (3) encourage small- and medium-sized enter-

7 prises and cooperative service providers to partici-

8 pate in investment activities in sub-Saharan Africa;

9 and

10   (4) publish measurable development impacts of

11 its investments.

12 (b) AMENDMENTS.—Title IV of chapter 2 of part I

13 of the Foreign Assistance Act of 1961 is amended—

14   (1) in section 233 (22 U.S.C. 2193)—

15   (A) in subsection (b), by inserting after the

16   sixth sentence the following new sentence: "Of

17   the eight such Directors, not more than six

18   should be of the same political party."; and

19   (B) by adding at the end the following new

20   subsection:

21 "(e) INVESTMENT ADVISORY COUNCIL.—The Board

22 shall take prompt measures to increase the loan, guar-

23 antee, and insurance programs, and financial commit-

24 ments, of the Corporation in sub-Saharan Africa, includ-

25 ing through the use of an investment advisory council to

1 assist the Board in developing and implementing policies,

2 programs, and financial instruments with respect to sub-

3 Saharan Africa. In addition, the investment advisory coun-

4 cil shall make recommendations to the Board on how the

5 Corporation can facilitate greater support by the United

6 States for trade and investment with and in sub-Saharan

7 Africa. The investment advisory council shall terminate on

8 December 31, 2017.";

9   (2) in section 234(c) (22 U.S.C. 2194(c)), by

10   inserting "eligible investors or" after "involve";

11   (3) in section 235(a)(2) (22 U.S.C. 2195), by

12   striking "2007" and inserting "2016"; and

13   (4) in section 239(c) (22 U.S.C. 2199(c)) to

14   read as follows:

15 "(e) INSPECTOR GENERAL.—The Board shall ap-

16 point and maintain an Inspector General in the Corpora-

17 tion, in accordance with the Inspector General Act of 1978

18 (5 U.S.C. App.).".

19   (c) POLICY.—Not later than 180 days after the date

20 of the enactment of this Act, the Board of Directors and

21 President of the Overseas Private Investment Corporation

22 are hereby directed to issue policy guidance that permits

23 significant investment in the electricity sector of the poor-

24 est and lowest pollution-emitting countries in a develop-

25 ment-driven and environmentally sensitive manner.

1 **SEC. 9. TRADE AND DEVELOPMENT AGENCY.**

2 (a) IN GENERAL.—The Director of the Trade and

3 Development Agency should—

4 (1) promote United States private sector par-

5 ticipation in energy sector development projects in

6 sub-Saharan Africa through project preparation ac-

7 tivities, including feasibility studies, technical assist-

8 ance, pilot projects, reverse trade missions, con-

9 ferences and workshops; and

10 (2) seek opportunities to fund project prepara-

11 tion activities that involve increased access to elec-

12 tricity, including power generation and trade capac-

13 ity building.

14 (b) FOCUS.—In pursuing the policy goals described

15 in section 4, project preparation activities described in

16 subsection (a) should focus on power generation using

17 clean energy sources, improving the efficiency of trans-

18 mission and distribution grids, including on-grid, off-grid

19 and mini-grid solutions, and promoting energy efficiency

20 and demand-side management.

21 **SEC. 10. PROGRESS REPORT.**

22 Not later than three years after the date of the enact-

23 ment of this Act, the President shall transmit to the Com-

24 mittee on Foreign Affairs of the House of Representatives

25 and the Committee on Foreign Relations of the Senate

1 a report on progress made toward achieving the policy

2 goals described in section 4, including the following:

3   (1) The number and type of policy and legisla-

4   tive changes implemented in partner countries to

5   support increased electricity generation and access

6   since United States engagement.

7   (2) A list of power sector and electrification

8   projects United States Government instruments are

9   supporting to achieve the policy goals described in

10   section 4, and for each such project—

11   (A) a description of how each such project

12   fits into the national power plans of the partner

13   country;

14   (B) the total cost of each such project and

15   predicted United States Government contribu-

16   tions to such projects broken down by United

17   States Government funding source, including

18   from the Overseas Private Investment Corpora-

19   tion, the United States Agency for International

20   Development, the Department of the Treasury,

21   and other appropriate United States Govern-

22   ment departments and agencies;

23   (C) the amount of actual United States

24   Government financing provided to such

25   projects, broken down by United States Govern-

1 ment funding source, including from the Over-

2 seas Private Investment Corporation, the

3 United States Agency for International Devel-

4 opment, the Department of the Treasury, and

5 other appropriate United States Government

6 departments and agencies;

7 (D) the predicted electrical power capacity

8 in megawatts of each project upon completion;

9 (E) expected environmental and social im-

10 pacts from each project;

11 (F) the number of individuals, businesses,

12 schools, and health facilities that have gained

13 electricity connections as a result of each

14 project at the time of such report;

15 (G) the predicted number of individuals

16 gaining electricity connections as a result of

17 each project upon completion; and

18 (H) the current operating electrical power

19 capacity in megawatts of each project.

○

AMENDMENT IN THE NATURE OF A SUBSTITUTE
TO H.R. 2548
OFFERED BY MR. ROYCE OF CALIFORNIA AND
MR. ENGEL OF NEW YORK

Strike all after the enacting clause and insert the following:

1 **SECTION 1. SHORT TITLE.**

2   This Act may be cited as the "Electrify Africa Act

3 of 2014".

4 **SEC. 2. PURPOSE.**

5   The purpose of this Act is to encourage the efforts

6 of countries in sub-Saharan Africa to improve access to

7 affordable and reliable electricity in Africa in order to

8 unlock the potential for economic growth, job creation,

9 food security, improved health, education and environ-

10 mental outcomes, and poverty reduction.

11 **SEC. 3. FINDINGS.**

12   Congress finds that—

13   (1) 589,000,000 people in sub-Saharan Africa,

14   or 68 percent of the population, did not have access

15   to electricity, as of 2010;

16   (2) in sub-Saharan Africa, electricity services

17   are highly unreliable and they are at least twice as

1   expensive for those with electricity access compared

2   to other emerging markets;

3   (3) lack of access to electricity services

4   disproportionally affects women and girls, who often

5   shoulder the burden of seeking sources of heat and

6   light such as dung, wood or charcoal and are often

7   more exposed to the associated negative health im-

8   pacts. Women and girls also face an increased risk

9   of assault from walking long distances to gather fuel

10   sources;

11   (4) access to electricity creates opportunities,

12   including entrepreneurship, for people to work their

13   way out of poverty;

14   (5) a lack of electricity contributes to the high

15   use of inefficient and often highly polluting fuel

16   sources for indoor cooking, heating, and lighting

17   that produce toxic fumes resulting in more than

18   3,000,000 annual premature deaths from respiratory

19   disease, more annual deaths than from HIV/AIDS

20   and malaria in sub-Saharan Africa;

21   (6) electricity access is crucial for the cold stor-

22   age of vaccines and anti-retroviral and other life-

23   saving medical drugs, as well as the operation of

24   modern lifesaving medical equipment;

1   (7) electricity access can be used to improve

2   food security by enabling post-harvest processing,

3   pumping, irrigation, dry grain storage, milling, re-

4   frigeration, and other uses;

5   (8) reliable electricity access can provide im-

6   proved lighting options and information and commu-

7   nication technologies, including Internet access and

8   mobile phone charging, that can greatly improve

9   health, social, and education outcomes, as well as

10   economic and commercial possibilities;

11   (9) sub-Saharan Africa's consumer base of

12   nearly one billion people is rapidly growing and will

13   create increasing demand for United States goods,

14   services, and technologies, but the current electricity

15   deficit in sub-Saharan Africa limits this demand by

16   restricting economic growth on the continent;

17   (10) approximately 30 African countries face

18   endemic power shortages, and nearly 70 percent of

19   surveyed African businesses cite unreliable power as

20   a major constraint to growth;

21   (11) the Millennium Challenge Corporation's

22   work in the energy sector shows high projected eco-

23   nomic rates of return that translate to sustainable

24   economic growth and that the highest returns are

25   projected when infrastructure improvements are cou-

1 pled with significant legislative, regulatory, institu-

2 tional, and policy reforms;

3   (12) in many countries, weak governance capac-

4 ity, regulatory bottlenecks, legal constraints, and

5 lack of transparency and accountability can stifle the

6 ability of private investment to assist in the genera-

7 tion and distribution of electricity; and

8   (13) without new policies and more effective in-

9 vestments in electricity sector capacity to increase

10 and expand electricity access in sub-Saharan Africa,

11 over 70 percent of the rural population, and 48 per-

12 cent of the total population, will potentially remain

13 without access to electricity by 2030.

14 **SEC. 4. STATEMENT OF POLICY.**

15 Congress declares that it is the policy of the United

16 States—

17   (1) in consultation with sub-Saharan African

18 governments, to encourage the private sector, inter-

19 national community, African Regional Economic

20 Communities, philanthropies, civil society, and other

21 governments to promote—

22   (A) the installation of at least an addi-

23   tional 20,000 megawatts of electrical power in

24   sub-Saharan Africa by 2020 to support poverty

1 reduction, promote development outcomes, and

2 drive economic growth;

3 (B) first-time direct access to electricity

4 for at least 50,000,000 people in sub-Saharan

5 Africa by 2020 in both urban and rural areas;

6 (C) efficient institutional platforms with

7 accountable governance to provide electrical

8 service to rural and underserved areas; and

9 (D) the necessary in-country legislative,

10 regulatory and policy reforms to make such ex-

11 pansion of electricity access possible; and

12 (2) to encourage private sector and inter-

13 national support for construction of hydroelectric

14 dams in sub-Saharan Africa that—

15 (A) offer low-cost clean energy consistent

16 with—

17 (i) the national security interests of

18 the United States; and

19 (ii) best international practices re-

20 garding social and environmental safe-

21 guards, including—

22 (I) engagement of local commu-

23 nities regarding the design, implemen-

24 tation, monitoring, and evaluation of

25 such projects;

1   (II) the consideration of energy

2   alternatives, including distributed re-

3   newable energy; and

4   (III) the development of appro-

5   priate mitigation measures; and

6   (B) support partner country efforts.

7 **SEC. 5. DEVELOPMENT OF A COMPREHENSIVE, MULTIYEAR**

8   **STRATEGY.**

9   (a) STRATEGY.—The President shall establish a com-

10 prehensive, integrated, multiyear policy, partnership, and

11 funding strategy to encourage countries in sub-Saharan

12 Africa to develop an appropriate mix of power solutions,

13 including renewable energy, to provide sufficient electricity

14 access to people living in rural and urban areas in order

15 to alleviate poverty and drive economic growth. Such strat-

16 egy shall maintain sufficient flexibility and remain respon-

17 sive to technological innovation in the power sector.

18   (b) REPORT.—

19   (1) IN GENERAL.—Not later than 180 days

20   after the date of the enactment of this Act, the

21   President shall transmit to the appropriate congres-

22   sional committees a report setting forth the strategy

23   described in subsection (a).

24   (2) REPORT CONTENTS.—The report required

25   by paragraph (1) shall include a discussion of the

1   elements described in paragraph (3), and should in-

2   clude a discussion of any additional elements rel-

3   evant to the strategy described in subsection (a).

4   (3) REPORT ELEMENTS.—The elements re-

5   ferred to in paragraph (2) are the following:

6   (A) The general and specific objectives of

7   the strategy described in subsection (a), the cri-

8   teria for determining success of the strategy, a

9   description of the manner in which the strategy

10   will support partner country efforts to increase

11   production and improve access to electricity,

12   and criteria and indicators used to select part-

13   ner countries for focused engagement on the

14   power sector.

15   (B) Development, by partner country gov-

16   ernments, of plans and regulations at the na-

17   tional, regional, and local level to increase

18   power production, strengthen existing electrical

19   transmission and distribution infrastructure,

20   bolster accountable governance and oversight,

21   and improve access to electricity.

22   (C) Administration plans to support part-

23   ner country efforts to increase new access to

24   electricity, including a description of how the

1   strategy will address commercial and residential

2   needs, as well as urban and rural access.

3   (D) Administration strategy to support

4   partner country efforts to reduce government

5   waste, fraud, and corruption, and improve exist-

6   ing power generation through improvement of

7   existing transmission and distribution systems,

8   as well as the use of a broad power mix, includ-

9   ing renewable energy, and the use of a distrib-

10   uted generation model.

11   (E) Administration policy to support part-

12   ner country efforts to attract private sector in-

13   vestment and public sector resources.

14   (F) A description of the Administration's

15   strategy for the transfer of relevant technology,

16   skills, and information to increase local partici-

17   pation in the long-term maintenance and man-

18   agement of the power sector to ensure invest-

19   ments are sustainable and transparent, includ-

20   ing details of the programs to be undertaken to

21   maximize United States contributions in the

22   areas of technical assistance and training.

23   (G) An identification of the relevant execu-

24   tive branch agencies that will be involved in car-

25   rying out the strategy, the level and distribution

1   of resources that will be dedicated on an annual

2   basis among such agencies, timely and com-

3   prehensive publication of aid information and

4   available transmission of resource data con-

5   sistent with Administration commitments to im-

6   plement the transparency measures specified in

7   the International Aid Transparency Initiative

8   by December 2015, the assignment of priorities

9   to such agencies, a description of the role of

10   each such agency, and the types of programs

11   that each such agency will undertake.

12   (H) A description of the mechanisms that

13   will be utilized by the Administration, including

14   the International Aid Transparency Initiative,

15   to coordinate the efforts of the relevant execu-

16   tive branch agencies in carrying out the strat-

17   egy to avoid duplication of efforts, enhance co-

18   ordination, and ensure that each agency under-

19   takes programs primarily in those areas where

20   each such agency has the greatest expertise,

21   technical capabilities, and potential for success.

22   (I) A description of the mechanisms that

23   will be established by the Administration for

24   monitoring and evaluating the strategy and its

25   implementation, including procedures for learn-

1 ing and sharing best practices among relevant

2 executive branch agencies, as well as among

3 participating countries, and for terminating un-

4 successful programs.

5   (J) A description of the Administration's

6 engagement plan, consistent with international

7 best practices, to ensure local and affected com-

8 munities are informed, consulted, and benefit

9 from projects encouraged by the United States,

10 as well as the environmental and social impacts

11 of the projects.

12   (K) A description of the mechanisms that

13 will be utilized to ensure greater coordination

14 between the United States and foreign govern-

15 ments, international organizations, African re-

16 gional economic communities, international

17 fora, the private sector, and civil society organi-

18 zations.

19   (L) A description of how United States

20 leadership will be used to enhance the overall

21 international response to prioritizing electricity

22 access for sub-Saharan Africa and to strength-

23 en coordination among relevant international

24 forums such as the Post-2015 Development

25 Agenda and the G8 and G20, as well as the

1   status of efforts to support reforms that are

2   being undertaken by partner country govern-

3   ments.

4   (M) An outline of how the Administration

5   intends to partner with foreign governments,

6   the international community, and other public

7   sector entities, civil society groups, and the pri-

8   vate sector to assist sub-Saharan African coun-

9   tries to conduct comprehensive project feasi-

10   bility studies and facilitate project development.

11   (N) A description of how the Administra-

12   tion intends to help facilitate transnational and

13   regional power and electrification projects

14   where appropriate.

15 **SEC. 6. USAID.**

16 (a) LOAN GUARANTEES.—It is the sense of Congress

17 that in pursuing the policy goals described in section 4,

18 the Administrator of USAID should identify and

19 prioritize—

20   (1) loan guarantees to local sub-Saharan Afri-

21   can financial institutions that would facilitate the in-

22   volvement of such financial institutions in power

23   projects in sub-Saharan Africa; and

1   (2) partnerships and grants for research, devel-

2 opment, and deployment of technology that would

3 increase access to electricity in sub-Saharan Africa.

4   (b) GRANTS.—It is the sense of Congress that the

5 Administrator of USAID should consider providing grants

6 to—

7   (1) support the development and implementa-

8 tion of national, regional, and local energy and elec-

9 tricity policy plans;

10   (2) expand distribution of electricity access to

11 the poorest; and

12   (3) build a country's capacity to plan, monitor

13 and regulate the energy and electricity sector.

14   (c) USAID DEFINED.—In this section, the term

15 "USAID" means the United States Agency for Inter-

16 national Development.

17 **SEC. 7. LEVERAGING INTERNATIONAL SUPPORT.**

18   In pursuing the policy goals described in section 4,

19 the President should direct the United States' representa-

20 tives to appropriate international bodies to use the influ-

21 ence of the United States, consistent with the broad devel-

22 opment goals of the United States, to advocate that each

23 such body—

24   (1) commit to significantly increase efforts to

25 promote investment in well-designed power sector

1 and electrification projects in sub-Saharan Africa

2 that increase energy access, in partnership with the

3 private sector and consistent with the host countries'

4 absorptive capacity;

5   (2) address energy needs of individuals and

6 communities where access to an electricity grid is

7 impractical or cost-prohibitive;

8   (3) enhance coordination with the private sector

9 in sub-Saharan Africa to increase access to elec-

10 tricity;

11   (4) provide technical assistance to the regu-

12 latory authorities of sub-Saharan African govern-

13 ments to remove unnecessary barriers to investment

14 in otherwise commercially viable projects; and

15   (5) utilize clear, accountable, and metric-based

16 targets to measure the effectiveness of such projects.

17 **SEC. 8. OVERSEAS PRIVATE INVESTMENT CORPORATION.**

18   (a) IN GENERAL.—The Overseas Private Investment

19 Corporation should—

20   (1) in carrying out its programs and pursuing

21 the policy goals described in section 4, place a pri-

22 ority on supporting investment in the electricity sec-

23 tor of sub-Saharan Africa, including renewable en-

24 ergy, and implement procedures for expedited review

25 of and, where appropriate, approval of, applications

1   by eligible investors for loans, loan guarantees, and

2   insurance for such investments;

3   (2) support investments in projects and partner

4   country strategies to the extent permitted by its au-

5   thorities, policies, and programs, that will—

6   (A) maximize the number of people with

7   new access to electricity to support economic

8   development;

9   (B) improve the generation, transmission,

10   and distribution of electricity;

11   (C) provide reliable and low-cost electricity,

12   including renewable energy and on-grid, off-

13   grid, and multi-grid solutions, to people living

14   in rural and urban communities;

15   (D) consider energy needs of individuals

16   where access to an electricity grid is impractical

17   or cost-prohibitive;

18   (E) reduce transmission and distribution

19   losses and improve end-use efficiency; and

20   (F) reduce energy-related impediments to

21   business and investment opportunity and suc-

22   cess;

23   (3) encourage locally-owned, micro, small- and

24   medium-sized enterprises and cooperative service

1 providers to participate in investment activities in

2 sub-Saharan Africa; and

3   (4) publish in an accessible digital format meas-

4 urable development impacts of its investments, in-

5 cluding appropriate quantifiable metrics to measure

6 energy access at the individual household, enterprise,

7 and community level; and

8   (5) publish in an accessible digital format the

9 amount, type, location, duration, and measurable re-

10 sults, with links to relevant reports and displays on

11 an interactive map, where appropriate, of all OPIC

12 investments and financings.

13 (b) AMENDMENTS.—Title IV of chapter 2 of part I

14 of the Foreign Assistance Act of 1961 is amended—

15   (1) in section 233 (22 U.S.C. 2193)—

16   (A) in subsection (b), by inserting after the

17 sixth sentence the following new sentence: "Of

18 the eight such Directors, not more than five

19 should be of the same political party."; and

20   (B) by adding at the end the following new

21 subsection:

22 "(c) INVESTMENT ADVISORY COUNCIL.—The Board

23 shall take prompt measures to increase the loan, guar-

24 antee, and insurance programs, and financial commit-

25 ments, of the Corporation in sub-Saharan Africa, includ-

34

1 ing through the use of an investment advisory council to

2 assist the Board in developing and implementing policies,

3 programs, and financial instruments with respect to sub-

4 Saharan Africa. In addition, the investment advisory coun-

5 cil shall make recommendations to the Board on how the

6 Corporation can facilitate greater support by the United

7 States for trade and investment with and in sub-Saharan

8 Africa. The investment advisory council shall terminate on

9 December 31, 2017.";

10   (2) in section 234(c) (22 U.S.C. 2194(c)), by

11   inserting "eligible investors or" after "involve";

12   (3) in section 235(a)(2) (22 U.S.C. 2195), by

13   striking "2007" and inserting "2017";

14   (4) in section 237(d) (22 U.S.C. 2197(d))—

15   (A) in paragraph (2), by inserting ", sys-

16   tems infrastructure costs," after "outside the

17   Corporation"; and

18   (B) in paragraph (3), by inserting ", sys-

19   tems infrastructure costs," after "project-spe-

20   cific transaction costs"; and

21   (5) by amending section 239(e) (22 U.S.C.

22   2199(c)) to read as follows:

23 "(e) INSPECTOR GENERAL.—The Board shall ap-

24 point and maintain an Inspector General in the Corpora-

1 tion, in accordance with the Inspector General Act of 1978

2 (5 U.S.C. App.).".

3 **SEC. 9. TRADE AND DEVELOPMENT AGENCY.**

4 (a) IN GENERAL.—The Director of the Trade and

5 Development Agency should—

6 (1) promote United States private sector par-

7 ticipation in energy sector development projects in

8 sub-Saharan Africa through project preparation ac-

9 tivities, including feasibility studies at the project,

10 sector, and national level, technical assistance, pilot

11 projects, reverse trade missions, conferences and

12 workshops; and

13 (2) seek opportunities to fund project prepara-

14 tion activities that involve increased access to elec-

15 tricity, including power generation and trade capac-

16 ity building.

17 (b) FOCUS.—In pursuing the policy goals described

18 in section 4, project preparation activities described in

19 subsection (a) should focus on power generation, including

20 renewable energy, improving the efficiency of transmission

21 and distribution grids, including on-grid, off-grid and

22 mini-grid solutions, and promoting energy efficiency and

23 demand-side management.

1 **SEC. 10. PROGRESS REPORT.**

2   Not later than three years after the date of the enact-

3 ment of this Act, the President shall transmit to the Com-

4 mittee on Foreign Affairs of the House of Representatives

5 and the Committee on Foreign Relations of the Senate,

6 and post through appropriate digital means, a report on

7 progress made toward achieving the policy goals described

8 in section 4, including the following:

9   (1) The number, type, and status of policy, reg-

10   ulatory, and legislative changes implemented in part-

11   ner countries to support increased electricity genera-

12   tion and access, and strengthen effective, account-

13   able governance of the electricity sector since United

14   States engagement.

15   (2) A list of power sector and electrification

16   projects United States Government instruments are

17   supporting to achieve the policy goals described in

18   section 4, and for each such project—

19   (A) a description of how each such project

20   fits into the national power plans of the partner

21   country;

22   (B) the total cost of each such project and

23   predicted United States Government contribu-

24   tions, and actual grants and other financing

25   provided to such projects, broken down by

26   United States Government funding source, in-

1   cluding from the Overseas Private Investment

2   Corporation, the United States Agency for

3   International Development, the Department of

4   the Treasury, and other appropriate United

5   States Government departments and agencies;

6   (C) the predicted electrical power capacity

7   of each project upon completion, with metrics

8   appropriate to the scale of electricity access

9   being supplied, as well as total megawatts in-

10 stalled;

11 (D) compliance with international best

12 practices and expected environmental and social

13 impacts from each project;

14 (E) the estimated number of women, men,

15 poor communities, businesses, schools, and

16 health facilities that have gained electricity con-

17 nections as a result of each project at the time

18 of such report; and

19 (F) the current operating electrical power

20 capacity in wattage of each project.

Amend the title so as to read: "A bill to establish
a comprehensive United States Government policy to encourage the efforts of countries in sub-Saharan Africa to
develop an appropriate mix of power solutions, including
renewable energy, for more broadly distributed electricity
access in order to support poverty reduction, promote de-

velopment outcomes, and drive economic growth, and for other purposes.".

Chairman ROYCE. Ladies and gentlemen, when we flip a light switch in this country, we power up a computer or swipe a credit card, we take for granted that the electricity that we are going to need to do that function is going to be there. But imagine for a moment if our shops or our schools or our hospitals and our homes had absolutely no electricity, what would happen if you flipped that switch and nothing happened? Even the most industrious manufacturer would be very hard pressed to stay in business. The most dedicated surgeon would be powerless in a hospital to save lives. And unfortunately, this is the reality throughout most of sub-Saharan Africa. Seventy percent of Africans lack access to dependable electricity.

The Electrify Africa Act is a response to this massive power shortage. It offers a market-based, strategic framework to bring affordable energy that is reliable to the 600 million people in sub-Saharan Africa who currently have none. Why do we care? We care because jobs are at stake, also human lives are at stake.

Now over all of Africa, the population is now about one billion. We have one billion consumers. The African continent has great economic potential. Last year, a bipartisan committee of a delegation here traveled to three countries, to Ghana, to Liberia, and Nigeria to see how these countries could make better use of the African Growth and Opportunity Act. I can tell you I and Greg Meeks have traveled in the past to these countries to see what could be done to create more economic growth. And we passed landmark legislation a decade ago in order to try to increase trade, increase opportunity, remove the barriers for exports from these countries to the U.S. But in all three of these countries, the production of goods for export was rendered nearly impossible by a lack of affordable energy, even where other countries in the region were doing well and where conditions were ripe for manufacturing, the problem is that the cost of running a plant on a diesel generator is simply prohibitive, not to mention the absence of electronic devices and Internet access now so critical to businesses and now very critical to education.

This lack of electricity even has a direct impact on our nation's spending. For example, the U.S. Embassy in Liberia spends—how much do you think they spend on their diesel generator there? $10,000 a day. That is why it is so impractical to think that small businesses are going to be set up to run and then have to rely on diesel generators. There is no usable grid in Liberia right now.

When I chaired the Africa Subcommittee, I saw first hand how a lack of electricity stifles development. Women spend long days searching for wood or searching for charcoal to provide heat for their families. Children study with light from highly flammable kerosene lamps and health risks are very high as a result. Cold storage of vaccines is almost impossible in this kind of a situation. Families resort to using inefficient and highly polluting sources of fuel and you can imagine what happens when the toxic fumes from those fuels waft through their homes. As a matter of fact, that causes more deaths in the region than HIV/AIDS and malaria combined.

Many of this committee have spent years working to help transition African countries away from assistance into economic growth. The Electrify Africa Act mandates a clear and comprehensive U.S. policy so that the private sector can proceed with the certainty it needs to generate electricity in Africa at no cost, by the way, to the U.S. taxpayer.

We need to be engaged. Where the United States has left a void for economic investment in Africa, China of course, steps in. China has directed $2 billion toward energy projects on the continent. If the United States wishes to tap into this potential consumer base, we must act now. So another point I would make for the members.

And I want to thank Ranking Member Eliot Engel and Africa Subcommittee Chair Chris Smith and Ranking Member Karen Bass, in particular, for helping craft this bill which comes at a crucial moment in time. And I want to also recognize the wide range of support for the bill from the 35 African Ambassadors who have sent letters of support to us here on Capitol Hill to the private sector groups like Chamber of Commerce and the Corporate Council of Africa and advocacy groups like the ONE Campaign and I would just like to ask those members of the ONE Campaign who are with us, if they would just stand for a moment to be recognized as well. Thank you very much for your engagement on this issue and the assistance in trying to electrify Africa.

And at the end of the day, I know the committee wants to see communities in sub-Saharan Africa flourish. This bill sets out a comprehensive, sustainable, market-based plan to bring hundreds of millions of Africans into the global economy. And I will now turn to our ranking member, Mr. Eliot Engel of New York for his opening statement.

Mr. ENGEL. Mr. Chairman, thank you for holding this markup of the Electrify Africa Act. I am very pleased and honored to be the lead Democratic cosponsor of this bipartisan legislation which addresses a critically important issue and let me say, did you ever see so many good looking, young people who stood up. I want to thank them for everything they are doing as well. It really makes me feel good when there are young people who are so involved. We have great hope for this country and for the future of the planet with young people being so heavily involved.

Mr. Chairman, sub-Saharan Africa is one of the most energy-deficient regions of the world with nearly 70 percent of the population which is more than half a billion people lacking access to electricity. In some countries that figure is even higher. In DRC, 85 percent of the population has no power; Kenya, 82 percent; Uganda, 92 percent. And those are really staggering statistics. The lack of reliable electricity has many negative consequences. In desperation, people burn anything they can find for heat and cooking: Wood, plastic, trash, and other toxic materials. These dirtier fuels cause greater harm to people's health and to the environment. Rural populations living off the grid require kerosene and cooking fuel to be transported from larger cities, making essential commodities cost more for those who are already struggling to survive.

Many businesses have had a hard time succeeding because they are forced to pour expensive diesel fuel into generators day and night or deal with constant power outages from unreliable electrical grids. Hospitals cannot provide adequate services because they are unable to provide consistent cold storage, light or power for life-saving devices and the list goes on and on.

This bill begins to tackle these challenges in a comprehensive way. It directs the Executive Branch to develop a strategy to increase electrification in Africa and to employ U.S. assistance programs to help accomplish that goal. This long-term strategy will focus not only on building more power plants, but also on increasing African Government accountability and transparency improving regulatory environments and increasing access to electricity in rural and poor communities through small, renewal energy projects.

Only by addressing all of these challenges together will people in Africa finally have access to electricity that will allow them to grow their economies and ultimately reduce their reliance on foreign aid.

Mr. Chairman, I know that you know sub-Saharan Africa is filled with dynamic individuals trying to make their countries better and I believe this bill supports their entrepreneurial spirit.

Mr. Chairman, our staffs have worked together in a bipartisan fashion which I am pleased to say has been the way we have run this committee. It has been a pleasure. We drafted this bill and refined it with a substitute now before us and we did it together. So Mr. Chairman, I appreciate your deep commitment to the people of sub-Saharan Africa and I look forward to working with you to move this bill forward. I yield back.

Chairman ROYCE. Thank you, Mr. Engel, very much. And thank you for your assistance also in drafting the legislation. We will go now to any members seeking to speak. We will go first to Mr. Chris Smith of New Jersey.

Mr. SMITH. Thank you very much, Mr. Chairman. Thank you, and Eliot Engel, for crafting this excellent bill, the Electrify Africa Act. Congress' interest in Africa is not only long standing and robust, but it is often varied. At times the focus is on peace and development, the mitigation of war. Sometimes it is more of an interest on trade. Others obviously, and all of us, I think, play a role in all of this. We believe education is the key to Africa's future success. And of course, humanitarian issues and combating of things like malaria, HIV/AIDS and TB are very, very high on the agenda. But you know, all of this and all of the progress is held back by the lack of electricity. And this legislation isn't a grant. It is not a brand new set of foreign aid initiatives. It calls for very serious cooperation and a strategy to electrify Africa, to use many of the advances we have made over the last several years with regards to electricity, best practices, of course, doing it in an environmentally sane and safe way letting us share that with Africa. Let us do it as partners. This legislation is an idea whose time has come and I thank the chairman for sponsoring it.

Chairman ROYCE. Thank you, Mr. Smith. We now go to Karen Bass of California.

Ms. BASS. Thank you, Chairman Royce and Ranking Member Engel for your hard work on this and I would like to associate myself with the comments of the ranking member Engel in terms of congratulating the chair on how the committee is run and the bipartisan way in which we have done legislation.

With greater access to electricity, Africa has the capacity to grow its economies, facilitating greater volumes of intra-regional, transcontinental, and international trade. Greater access to electricity also enables countries to expand human capacity and address the critical challenges of under employment. Access to additional power will also help both individual countries and geographic regions address infrastructure challenges, all of which contribute to increasing the capacity of African nations and the continent as a whole.

Greater access to electricity improves the quality of life for not only urban, but rural communities. In the absence of electricity, the ability to work, to run a household, or to do homework after dark is truly a challenging feat, especially in rural areas. Many of you may have heard the inspiring story of the young Kenyan engineering student, Mr. Evans Wadongo, one of CNN's top heroes of 2010, who at the age of 19 literally transformed the lives of people in his village by developing a solar lamp. Ask why he spent so much time and money attempting to produce the lamp, Mr. Wadongo said he did so to improve the lives of people like himself and to ensure that no other student had to go through what he had to go through just to study.

Mr. Wadongo's eyesight is permanently damaged due to prolonged use of kerosene lamps and the irritation of his eyes from kerosene fumes. Reportedly, Mr. Wadongo hopes to produce some 100,000 solar lamps by 2015. His story underscores the importance of balanced access to electrical power and the need to ensure that power is not simply directed to the economic sectors, but also to the rural and low-income communities where many bright students like Mr. Wadongo live.

I think for all of us, it is very hard to imagine what it would be like to go through a day without electricity. I often think of the health challenges that this presents and the number of women on the continent who have to deliver children in the dark.

In closing, I want to acknowledge the concerns raised by a number of organizations and express my appreciation to your staff, Mr. Chairman, for meeting with all of the advocacy groups and taking their concerns into consideration. I understand that their concerns are that renewables be included, that access to electricity be for the general population, and that we make sure that governance of the infrastructure is transparent. I yield back the balance of my time.

Chairman ROYCE. Thank you, Congresswoman Bass. We will now go to Congressman Duncan of South Carolina.

Mr. DUNCAN. I want to thank the chairman. You know, this is an interesting bill to me, being a pro-energy guy and thinking about improving the quality of lives for folks all around the globe, specifically in Africa today, but we can incorporate most third world countries and how do we improve the lives of folks that are using charcoal to cook with or wood or coal to heat their homes. Electricity does that.

Electricity provides a way to keep food from spoiling for a long time. Electricity provides an ability for third world parents to educate their children and help them read after the sun goes down. It provides the air quality improvement. If you are cooking and heating with combustible products like coal or charcoal or wood, air quality is not as good.

So I am supportive of this effort. But I want to mention to the committee one thing that I would hope the administration in embracing this bill would consider and that is small, modular reactors which is a new technology, but new to this day, but not new to the nuclear industry. It has been around a long time. Small modular reactors can power small cities, large neighborhoods, and in this case in Africa, small villages with a very stable 24/7 baseload power supply to meet the needs of the electrical components there.

And if you think about—and I think about the African villages, but also the manufacturing processes that could come in to provide incomes and stability, I think about the moms and dads having fresh food in their refrigerators and cooking over electric stoves and that sort of thing. So there are a lot of things to think about when we think about electricity in third world countries and transmission lines and security and other things, especially with regard to small modular reactors that I know others that may not like nuclear power will raise the concern about proliferation of nuclear materials, but there are ways that can be used in that area.

So I would hope that the administration would look at small modular reactors as a viable source and it is not all just hydro power. There are other ways that we can meet the needs. I think this is the right thing to try to support electrifying Africa and all of the third world to bring them up in their standard of liver and quality of life. And with that, Mr. Chairman, I yield back.

Chairman ROYCE. Thank you. We go now to Mr. Meeks of New York.

Mr. MEEKS. Thank you, Mr. Chairman. First, I want to join Mr. Engel and Ms. Bass in congratulating you. This is not new for you. You have been working to make sure that Africa receives the kind of investments and infrastructure from the time that you were the chair of the Subcommittee on Africa and you have conducted yourself here in a manner to make sure that that has become a reality. And so I want to thank you for your hard work and your diligence on this particular bill.

I want to thank Ranking Member Engel who has consistently and constantly been working very hard to work in a bipartisan manner, making sure that his contributions to you and the way he listens and talks to members on our side of the rise on this committee. That makes this happen and that makes these things work. So I want to thank Mr. Engel and Mr. Smith, who is always on humanitarian causes and works hard in doing what he has to do. And in regards to this bill, I want to thank you, because it is a joint effort.

And of course, my friend and colleague, Karen Bass, who I think of two things. Number one, I also think of my good friend who is looking down from heaven, Donald Payne, who had worked so hard and so tremendously for a long period of time on working on Africa and trying to see this happen and then the baton being passed to Karen Bass, who in her vision, says that we are going to work and she was going to work just as hard as Donald did. And every time I look up, there is something in my hand about Africa that Karen is producing to make sure that Africa is on the thoughts and the minds and the hearts of everybody. So I want to thank you.

And of course, I want to thank Mr. Bono and the ONE Campaign who decided to utilize his celebrity to make sure it becomes on the lips of a lot of individuals. Sometimes if you don't have a celebrity, what is going on in other parts of the world no one knows about. But the ONE Campaign and Mr. Bono decided that they were going to stay focused on this and bring the attention to the world. And that then also gives us the motivation on the committee to make sure that we get something and we do something right. And I think that is what we are doing here today. So I want to thank them.

I am so excited to see that the committee takes this proactive action to increase U.S. engagement and investment in Africa. You know, years ago when one would discuss Africa often we only heard it characterized as the poorest continent on the planet. That is no longer the case. More often you hear about flourishing economic progress today. Six out of the top ten fastest growing economies in the world are in sub-Saharan Africa. Over the past decade it has been a six-fold increase in U.S. and foreign direct investment in sub-Saharan Africa to $39.5 billion.

On June 30, 2013, in a speech in Capetown, South Africa, President Barack Obama remarked, ''There is a historic shift taking place from poverty to growing, massive middle class.'' Africa has a great story to tell, but more needs to be done for Africa to reach its full potential. Investments and key infrastructure such as reliable energy are vital to continuing African growth and development.

President Obama's Power Africa initiative capitalizes on the progress by leveraging international support, the private sector, and regional cooperation to dramatically increase electricity across Africa. The Electrify Africa Act will solidify ambitious goals for low cost, clean energy on the continent, including 20,000 megawatts of electrical power by 2020.

I have hosted various seminars and trade events to encourage trade and investment in Africa. The Electrify Africa Act of 2014 will bring the kind of confidence to investors that Africa has the capacity to support long-term economic growth and is a stable partner for private corporations, NGOs, international organizations, and entrepreneurs. Through this bill, more effective investments in the electricity sector will further enhance Africa's trade capacity. And it will give children the ability to learn; hospitals, the opportunity to heal; families, the opportunity to come together; create jobs and opportunities for those who had none.

I look forward to working with my colleagues on this committee to ensure Africa's future continues to be as bright as the sun. Thank you, and I yield back.

Chairman ROYCE. Thank you very much. We go now to Mr. Mo Brooks of Alabama.

Mr. BROOKS. Mr. Chairman and members of the committee, I very much appreciate the altruistic motivations that I have heard in support of this legislation, but quite frankly I don't believe America's financial condition is such that it supports spending this money that we don't have on these projects. The realities of America's financial condition, quite frankly, are rather dire. Over the past 5 years we have averaged trillion-dollar deficits every single year. That has been our average. To put that in a different perspective, I would ask the members and the audience to think in terms of their personal finances. How long could each of us stay out of bankruptcy if year after year after year for 5 consecutive years, 30 percent of our operational costs, what we spent to live on, was borrowed money? Yet that is the financial condition of the United States of America over the past 5 years.

We have economic history that we can look at that tells us what the dire consequences are going to be if we continue on this path. You can look at Detroit and Stockton, major cities in the United States of America. They are in bankruptcy because of this tendency to spend money that you don't have which politicians are also apt to do. Now in Detroit, they are bailing in bankruptcy whether retirees of the City of Detroit are going to receive the pensions that they earned during their lifetimes and that they now need during their elderly years.

We can look at Spain and Greece, again, a couple of governments who have not had financial constraint and who have been spending money that they do not have. Their unemployment rate right now exceeds 25 percent in both of those nations. Now think about that for a moment. Those are unemployment rates because of financial irresponsibility that are worse than at any point in time during America's Great Depression of the 1930s.

You can look at Argentina and Venezuela if you want more examples of the consequences of the path that we are on, where in 1 month their currency was devalued anywhere from 17, 18 percent on the low side to roughly 50 percent on the high side in 1 month. Of course, you are going to have economic adverse consequences from that or you can look at Puerto Rico, a part of the United States, which just 2 weeks ago Fitch downgraded their sovereign debt to junk bond status.

Puerto Rico is going to be suffering for years, if not decades, because of the financial irresponsibility of their leadership or they didn't properly prioritize and where they didn't say no to good things, not because they don't want to do those good things, but because they don't have the money with which to do those good things.

Let us be clear then. Every penny that is spent by America on building power plants and power lines in Africa is borrowed. It is money we do not have and money we do not have the ability to pay back. That having been said, there is some issue about whether this bill is going to cost American taxpayers money. I would direct everyone to Section 6 of the bill which is page 11 where we are going to be guaranteeing loans: "USAID should identify and prioritize loan guarantees to local sub-Saharan African financial institutions.'' That is money that the United States of America is on the hook for.

If you go to the very next paragraph, it is talking about partnerships and grants, again, taxpayer money that would have to be spent. If you want to look at Section 8 on page 13, the Overseas Private Investment Corporation, which by the way we appropriated $55 million for in FY 2012 and the President is asking for $72 million in 2014 in his budget proposal. That also is going to be assisting with investments that in turn cost money ultimately that may be American taxpayer money.

Before I go any further, let me emphasize, USAID does not come cheap. We are talking $17 billion FY 2014, $17 billion. That is how much that is costing American taxpayers. Or if you want to go to Section 9, Director of Trade and Development, page 17 again, this one is talking about, if you will bear with me while I get to that page, ''the Director of Trade and Development Agency should promote United States private sector participation in energy sector development.'' That is administration. That is going to cost money for us to do that. ''Seek opportunities to fund project preparation activities including power generation.'' There is a whole slew of things that are going to cost, but the bottom line is this, there is no way that anyone can say that this is not going to cost American taxpayers money. It is. Money that we don't have.

You can make the argument that the money is going to be spent anyways, and that we ought to spend it on this program which is a separate argument. But I would submit in response that once you lock this legislation in it is going to be very difficult to cut the funding to conform to the financial circumstances that we face as a nation. So I admire the altruism that is expressed so far. I regret that because of our nation's financial condition I cannot support spending American taxpayer dollars on power lines and power plants in Africa.

Chairman ROYCE. To recognize myself, of course, what this bill is about is giving the private sector in the United States the certainty it needs to go in and create in Africa products that are American-made products that create American jobs over the Overseas Private Investment Corporation. And if we go through the scoring of the CBO, this, in fact, is a proposal that not only does not cost, this is one of the few proposals that we are going to pass that actually is scored to bring revenues into the Federal coffers here in the United States. Why is that so? Because when you give American companies the certainty that they can go and invest, they do so. They create the synergy of the new jobs and the new economic relationship and to put this in context, this is something of a race in Africa between the private sector, the U.S. going in and investing, and China going in and investing in a very different way.

When the U.S. goes in, we have a certain template that we are attempting to sell here, market economy, an open economy, not sole sourcing products, but opening up to the international market. The rule of law becomes part of this because over AGOA, this is part of the thesis of what we do when we engage with African states, recognizing the rule of law, recognizing an independent court system, and now providing energy, uninterrupted energy in order to be able to entice additional U.S. investment in the subcontinent.

So at the end of the day, when we look at the CBO report and it shows a return of tens of millions of dollars on these projects, I would argue that this is a very wise investment for the United States to make. And I know Mr. Sherman seeks recognition from California, thank you.

Mr. SHERMAN. I want to associate myself with the chairman's opening statement and just about everything else that has been said there. In response to the gentleman from Alabama, as the chairman points out, this bill has no additional cost. We have an obligation to spend our foreign development dollars as effectively as possible and I am proud to be one of many cosponsors of this bill because this bill will help us be more efficient.

It involves using existing loan guarantee authority, encouraging the World Bank and the African Development Bank to use their dollars to focus on electricity. And as to the Overseas Private Investment Corporation, we have had hearings in our subcommittee on this. As a technical matter, $72 million is appropriated this year or will be under the President's request, but that is a bookkeeping entry.

Over the years, the Overseas Private Investment Corporation has returned more money to the Treasury than it has received. And I am confident that the guarantee fees that it will charge to guarantee debt to finance projects, to electrify Africa will again be part of their success in earning a profit for the United States Treasury.

So even if one is not an enthusiastic supporter of foreign aid, I happen to be, but not everyone is, this bill represents the very efficient use of a small amount of money that would be spent anyway to do something that is important for Africa as well, illustrated in the comments here and also very important for African global trade. I yield back.

Chairman ROYCE. Yes, if the gentleman yields back, I would point out that what we are actually talking about here is a template. For some time now, this country has been moving away from aid, the U.S. has been moving away from aid to trade with Africa. But to now say that we are going to move away from trade and investment in Africa with respect to the OPIC template which again is giving U.S. firms the security they need to go in, they are paying fees. And I just want the members to understand this. The fees that the companies pay to go in in order to make these investments is what covers the cost. And the structure of that fee system is such that according to the Congressional Budget Office, there is a return on investment. In other words, there is net revenues flowing in going forward to the U.S. Treasury when contrasted with the expenditures. It is a net revenue of tens of millions of dollars.

So with that said, let me recognize who is next in the queue and that is Mr. Gerry Connolly of Virginia.

Mr. CONNOLLY. I thank the chairman, and I associate myself with his remarks. I also thank our colleague from Alabama, Mr. Brooks, for giving voice to the alternative view of the United States' role in the world. What he basically said was the goals contained in the markup today and the legislation today an the markup are altruistic and worthy in that regard, but we can't afford them.

This zero sum gain view of the United States' role in the world, I would argue, is very dangerous. It is a false choice to tell the American people we cannot continue to afford to be engaged in the world. And even when things are financed, self-financed, we still can't afford them in that point of view. In fact, we need to retreat.

I find it ironic that electrification in Africa, for example, is referred to as an altruistic endeavor. Indeed, Mr. Brooks' own home state of Alabama was a prime beneficiary of rural electrification during the New Deal. And I am sure his constituents are grateful that a different administration at a time of far greater economic stress than today, made that investment in his citizens, in his state, in his economy. And the return on that investment has been profound.

When we talk a zero sum gain about the United States retreating from the world, we give up on the idea that an investment can have a return on it. When the United States makes an investment in other people, in other places, it is not only altruism, I would say to my colleague, it is also enlightened self-interest because the return in terms of economic activity, in terms of trade, in terms of investment both ways, is going to be considerable. It is a minor investment relative to the return we are going to see in 20 or 30 years' time. It is not just altruism. It is also enlightened self-interest.

And in fact, I would argue it is about our own future and our children's future because as the chairman indicated, if we don't do it, there are others more than willing to make those investments because they do see the return, the Chinese chief among them. And I don't want to be the person who has to answer the next generation why is the Africa-Chinese trade the dominant trade in that part of the world and we don't even have a slice of it? And the answer is because somebody, somewhere 20 years before said because we can't afford it. It is a false choice and I hope this committee will reject that choice, although I commend my colleague for making it quite clear what that choice is. With that, I yield back, Mr. Chairman.

Chairman ROYCE. We now go to Mr. Ted Yoho of Florida.

Mr. YOHO. Thank you, Mr. Chairman, and my sentiments were similar to Mr. Brooks in the beginning, but as I studied this, when you see OPIC, OPIC has a self-sustaining basis at no net cost to the American taxpayers. It is generated net profits of $272 million on Fiscal Year 2012 which has helped reduce the Federal budget deficit for the 35th consecutive year in a row.

And today, OPIC has supported nearly 200 billion of investment in more than 4,000 projects around the world and it has generated $75 billion in U.S. exports and supported more than 277,000 American jobs. And I have been looking for a way and I know this committee has and I do commend you for the leadership you have had and the bipartisan support we have had on this committee of a way to have a paradigm shift in our foreign aid. And if this is a way that we can invest and not give aid to corrupt governments, but invest and it generates money to the American taxpayers, I am in support of it. And I yield back. Thank you.

48

Chairman ROYCE. Do any other members seek—oh, yes. Mr. Cicilline. Sorry, sir.

Mr. CICILLINE. Thank you, Mr. Chairman. I, too, would like to begin by recognizing and thanking you and Ranking Member Engel for the bipartisan way in which you have approached this important issue and for continuing to educate members of this committee and the general public on the importance of supporting the energy sector in Africa.

I would also like to acknowledge the contributions of our subcommittee chair, Congressman Smith, and the passionate and determined and relentless advocacy and leadership of our Ranking Member Karen Bass who has been such a strong advocate, not only for this piece of legislation but for so many issues important to Africa.

In sub-Saharan Africa, almost 600 million people do not have access to electricity. This, of course, presents challenges not only to quality of life, but also health, educational opportunities, and safety. In particular, women and girls are at greater risk of physical violence without street lamps and phones. And many children are not able to attend school because they are needed to complete tasks at home and those who are lucky enough to go to school, often can't study in the evenings after the sun goes down. And their health outcome and wellness are compromised as many have mentioned without electricity.

In addition to the obvious impact on quality of life, it is also critical that energy be provided if the full potential of Africa is to be realized. According to the African Development Bank, Africa's economy is growing faster than that of any other continent. At the same time, in 2012, USAID assistance to 42 African countries totaled $8.1 billion. We cannot expect African countries to be able to fully take ownership of their own successes and failures and reach their full growth potential until and unless they establish basic dependable and comprehensive infrastructure.

A coordinated U.S. strategy to improve access to modern electricity will boost African economic growth and security. It will also increase U.S. investment in a rapidly-growing continent. And I am proud to be one of many cosponsors of this act and really just want to end by saying that this is an action that is not only in the best interest of the countries on the continent, but also in the best interest of the national security interest of our country and the long-term economic well-being of this country. I urge my colleagues to support its passage. And with that, I yield back.

Chairman ROYCE. Thank you, Mr. Cicilline. We go now to Mr. Meadows of North Carolina.

Mr. MEADOWS. Thank you, Mr. Chairman, and thank you for your leadership as well as Ranking Member Engel. I have had the opportunity to work with Ms. Bass on this particular issue as well and so my hats off to so many.

In an environment where fiscal—as my good friend from Alabama, he and I both share our concerns over the fiscal responsibility of our Government. I would like to point out and associate my remarks with my good friend from Florida, Mr. Yoho. OPIC is one of the few things, one of the few agencies within the Federal Government that actually provides a return.

49

And if you look at some of the most difficult times in terms of foreign governments, either in North Africa or the Middle East, in terms of having a difficult time with the political stability, even in spite of that environment, since 2009, OPIC has returned over $800 million to the general Treasury. So if in the most difficult of times they can provide a positive return, I think that it is the kind of risk as a small business owner that I would love to have that model to continue to work, providing return to general Treasury.

And as we start to work these things together, I have met with Ambassadors from all over Africa. And their big concern quite frankly is is that America is not playing and not investing in African countries like China is. And if we are going to compete globally we need to unleash the private sector to allow them to invest in these countries in a real and full way, and embrace the kind of relationship that we have with many of our friends in Africa.

And so I wholeheartedly support this bill and appreciate the work of so many in leadership who have moved this bill forward. And you can count on my support. I yield back.

Chairman ROYCE. I thank the gentleman. Any other members seeking recognition. If not, are there any amendments to the base text?

Mr. Meadows, do you have an amendment at the desk?

Mr. MEADOWS. Thank you, Mr. Chairman, I do have an amendment at the desk.

Chairman ROYCE. Than I will ask the Clerk to read that amendment.

Ms. MARTER. Amendment to the amendment in the nature of a substitute to H.R. 2548 offered by Mr. Meadows of North Carolina. Page 17 after line 2, insert the following: See annual consumer satisfaction survey and report, one survey, a, in general, for each of calendar years 2014 through 2016, the Overseas Private Investment Corporation shall conduct a survey of private entities that sponsor or are involved in projects that are insured, reinsured, guaranteed or financed by the Corporation regarding the level of satisfaction of such entities with the operations and procedures of the Corporation with respect to such projects.

[The information referred to follows:]

AMENDMENT TO THE AMENDMENT IN THE NATURE OF A SUBSTITUTE TO H.R. 2548 OFFERED BY MR. MEADOWS OF NORTH CAROLINA

Page 17, after line 2, insert the following:

1   (c) ANNUAL CONSUMER SATISFACTION SURVEY AND
2 REPORT.—

3   (1) SURVEY.—

4   (A) IN GENERAL.—For each of calendar
5   years 2014 through 2016, the Overseas Private
6   Investment Corporation shall conduct a survey
7   of private entities that sponsor or are involved
8   in projects that are insured, reinsured, guaran-
9   teed, or financed by the Corporation regarding
10   the level of satisfaction of such entities with the
11   operations and procedures of the Corporation
12   with respect to such projects.

13   (B) PRIORITY.—The survey shall be pri-
14   marily focused on United States small busi-
15   nesses and businesses that sponsor or are in-
16   volved in projects with a cost of less than
17        $20,000,000 (as adjusted for inflation).

18   (2) REPORT.—

51

1   (A) IN GENERAL.—Not later than each of

2   July 1, 2015, July 1, 2016, and July 1, 2017,

3   the Corporation should submit to the congres-

4   sional committees specified in subparagraph (C)

5   a report on the results of the survey required

6   under paragraph (1).

7   (B) MATTERS TO BE INCLUDED.—The re-

8   port should include the Corporation's plans to

9   revise its operations and procedures based on

10   concerns raised in the results of the survey, if

11   appropriate.

12   (C) FORM.—The report shall be submitted

13   in unclassified form and shall not disclose any

14   confidential business information.

15   (D) CONGRESSIONAL COMMITTEES SPECI-

16   FIED.—The congressional committees specified

17   in this subparagraph are—

18   (i) the Committee on Appropriations

19   and the Committee on Foreign Affairs of

20   the House of Representatives; and

21   (ii) the Committee on Appropriations

22   and the Committee on Foreign Relations

23   of the Senate.

Mr. MEADOWS. Mr. Chairman, could I move that this amendment be considered read?

Chairman ROYCE. Without objection. The Chair reserves a point of order and recognizes the author to briefly explain his amendment.

Mr. MEADOWS. Thank you, Mr. Chairman. This is a very simple amendment that really becomes a tool to hopefully allow the Overseas Private Investment Corporation to conduct annual surveys to report back to this committee and other appropriate committees within Congress in terms of the level of satisfaction, potential problems, or potential improvements that might be suggested either that they have taken or that we might consider legislatively to improve really the focus on small businesses. It only pertains to those small businesses or businesses that are sponsored with projects that cost less than $20 million. It just provides an issue where we can start to evaluate the effectiveness of this program and be a more effective body here in terms of addressing the needs and making it streamlined in terms of the return that I previously spoke about, hopefully making that one that we can count on on a regular basis going forward and with that I would be open to answer any questions.

Chairman ROYCE. Do any members seek recognition to speak on the amendment? Yes, Mr. Grayson of Florida.

Mr. GRAYSON. Thanks. If I understand this amendment properly, what it is is it is depicting as a consumer satisfaction survey a survey of entities who benefit from OPIC as it is used in the term here in the amendment, private entities that sponsor or are involved in projects with OPIC. I am not sure that is a good idea. I don't think that resembles people's conventional view of what a consumer satisfaction survey is.

Also, I am concerned about the potential cost of this. OPIC operates at a profit, in part, because it is not tied down by what amounts to an unfunded mandate like this one. I haven't heard any discussion yet of what this would cost. If we load down OPIC with unfunded mandates, then presumably OPIC will stop being profitable.

I have some points of order that I would like to raise, Mr. Chairman. Should I raise them now during this time or wait until debate is over?

Chairman ROYCE. I think now might be the time, Mr. Grayson, that you want to raise any point of order you might have.

Mr. GRAYSON. Thank you, Mr. Chairman. First, I am concerned about the germaneness of this amendment, both with regard to Rule 5(b)(3) and in general. I note that this amendment doesn't contain the word Africa, nor the word electricity in it. It may be a good idea on its own. I tend to think not. But this seems to me to be something that is properly presented to committee as a stand-alone bill and is not germane to Electrify Africa Act.

Chairman ROYCE. If I could respond to that point at this moment, Mr. Grayson?

Mr. GRAYSON. yes.

Chairman ROYCE. In my consultation here with the parliamentarian, he tells me that because of the subject in Section 8 of the base text, this amendment is germane. The rationale is this. The subject in the base text speaks to the issue of OPIC as a whole in sections of that language, but not exclusively to African electrification. So it would be germane under that reading.

Mr. GRAYSON. Well, Mr. Chairman, I would also like to raise a point of order concerning this being a second order amendment. We are now looking at amendment to the amendment in the nature of a substitute. Does the committee entertain second, third, and fourth order amendments?

Chairman ROYCE. Let me give you again the parliamentarian's view on this. The Meadows amendment is subject to second degree amendment because the amendment in the nature of a substitute is base text rather than an amendment.

Mr. GRAYSON. Can the chairman clarify that further for future reference?

Chairman ROYCE. The ANS is base text as though it was the introduced text of the bill itself. So it is not an amendment. And I think that is usually the way an amendment in the nature of a substitute, once it is accepted is treated.

Mr. GRAYSON. Mr. Chairman, that raises an interesting general point and I am asking now not just for this context, but for future reference, does that mean that an amendment in the nature of a substitute is counted as base text whether or not it meets the 48-hour notice rule?

Chairman ROYCE. It did meet the 48-hour notice rule.

Mr. GRAYSON. If it had not met the 48-hour notice rule, would that still be the case?

Chairman ROYCE. We would not, under committee rules in that situation put it as base text. We would have to consider it instead as an amendment.

Mr. GRAYSON. Thank you, Mr. Chairman, that is very helpful and will be interesting in future context. I would also like to raise a point of order concerning the committee's jurisdiction over this particular amendment, both with regard to the fact that it applies to OPIC as a stand-alone and that it seems to involve the expenditure of appropriated funds.

Chairman ROYCE. Well, yes, according to the House parliamentarian, OPIC is within, clearly, the jurisdiction of this committee. We have authority oversight over OPIC and jurisdiction over OPIC. So the amendment would be in order.

Mr. GRAYSON. All right, thank you for those rulings. I will continue to object to this amendment on the basis that it amounts to an unfunded mandate against OPIC and should have properly been brought as a stand-alone bill for the committee's perusal and not as a last-minute amendment. Thank you. I yield back.

Chairman ROYCE. I thank the gentleman for yielding. Do other members wish to seek recognition to speak on this amendment?

The Chair withdraws the point of order and I would point out to just recognize myself for a minute, OPIC is already doing much of what is requested I think in this amendment. And I wonder, returning to the author of the amendment, Mr. Meadows, would you like to respond?

Mr. MEADOWS. You know, I enjoy a good relationship and wholeheartedly support the efforts of OPIC and have worked with them both privately and certainly encouraging other members to support not only their efforts, but the efforts in general to promote overseas private investment. This particular function becomes something that would make this a function of an obligatory requirement to report annually to Congress on efforts that they are taking, something that quite frankly under the current leadership that they are doing now, however, with change of the administration and the potential change in leadership within that particular corporation, that could change. And so this promotes an activity that I think that we are enjoying now and more codifies it and makes it official. Thank you, Mr. Chairman.

Chairman ROYCE. For my remaining time, upon some reflection, I think the survey, arguably, would then require OPIC to provide some information here that might be pretty useful, that could help improve their operation and their relevance to small business and of course, at the end of the day, small business remains the largest employer in the United States. So from that standpoint, this information could be useful and I am told that they do surveys currently.

So my presumption is that this would fit within the framework of what they are currently doing without tremendous additional cost, but probably with the added benefit of being useful to small business in the United States. And from that standpoint, I am prepared to support the amendment and appreciate the gentleman's effort. But if there is no further request for recognition, the question will occur on Mr. Meadows' amendment.

All of those in favor say aye.

All those opposed say no.

In the opinion of the Chair, the ayes have it. The amendment is agreed to and we will go now to a recorded vote. Let me also—without objection, H.R. 2548, as amended. Hearing no further amendments to this measure, the question occurs on agreeing to H.R. 2548, as amended. All those in favor say aye.

All those opposed, no.

In the opinion of the Chair, the ayes have it. The bill, as amended, is agreed to. Without objection, H.R. 2548 is ordered favorably reported. It will be reported as a single amendment in the nature of a substitute. Staff is directed to make any technical and conforming changes and that concludes business for today.

I want to thank Ranking Member Engel and all of our committee members for their constitutions and assistance to today's markup. And in addition, I would like to thank Nilmini Rubin. I would like to thank our other staff members here, Worku Gachou and Jackie Quinones for their support on this legislation. Thank you very much. We stand adjourned.

[Whereupon, at 11:01 a.m., the committee was adjourned.]

APPENDIX

———

MATERIAL SUBMITTED FOR THE RECORD

FULL COMMITTEE MARKUP NOTICE
COMMITTEE ON FOREIGN AFFAIRS
U.S. HOUSE OF REPRESENTATIVES
WASHINGTON, DC 20515-6128

Edward R. Royce (R-CA), Chairman

February 27, 2014

TO: MEMBERS OF THE COMMITTEE ON FOREIGN AFFAIRS

You are respectfully requested to attend an OPEN meeting of the Committee on Foreign Affairs, to be held in Room 2172 of the Rayburn House Office Building (and available live on the Committee website at http://www.ForeignAffairs.house.gov):

DATE: Thursday, February 27, 2014

TIME: 10:00 a.m.

MARKUP OF: H.R. 2548, Electrify Africa Act of 2013

By Direction of the Chairman

The Committee on Foreign Affairs seeks to make its facilities accessible to persons with disabilities. If you are in need of special accommodations, please call 202/225-5021 at least four business days in advance of the event, whenever practicable. Questions with regard to special accommodations in general (including availability of Committee materials in alternative formats and assistive listening devices) may be directed to the Committee.

COMMITTEE ON FOREIGN AFFAIRS
MINUTES OF FULL COMMITTEE MARKUP

Day___ *Thursday*___ Date___ *02/27/14*___ Room___ *2172*___

Starting Time ___ *10:06 P.M.*___ Ending Time ___ *11:01 A.M.*___

Recesses __*0*__ (___to___) (___to___) (___to___) (___to___) (___to___) (___to___)

Presiding Member(s)
Rep. Edward R. Royce, Chairman

Check all of the following that apply:

Open Session ☑   Electronically Recorded (taped) ☑
Executive (closed) Session ☐   Stenographic Record ☑
Televised ☑

BILLS FOR MARKUP: *(Include bill number(s) and title(s) of legislation.)*
H.R. 2548

COMMITTEE MEMBERS PRESENT:
See Attendance Sheet.

NON-COMMITTEE MEMBERS PRESENT:
None.

STATEMENTS FOR THE RECORD: *(List any statements submitted for the record.)*
None.

ACTIONS TAKEN DURING THE MARKUP: *(Attach copies of legislation and amendments.)*
See Markup Summary.

RECORDED VOTES TAKEN (FOR MARKUP): *(Attach final vote tally sheet listing each member.)*

Subject	Yeas	Nays	Present	Not Voting

TIME SCHEDULED TO RECONVENE _____
or
TIME ADJOURNED *11:01 A.M.*

Doug Anderson, General Counsel

HOUSE COMMITTEE ON FOREIGN AFFAIRS
FULL COMMITTEE MARKUP

PRESENT	MEMBER	PRESENT	MEMBER
X	Edward R. Royce, CA	X	Eliot L. Engel, NY
X	Christopher H. Smith, NJ		Eni F.H. Faleomavaega, AS
	Ileana Ros-Lehtinen, FL	X	Brad Sherman, CA
X	Dana Rohrabacher, CA	X	Gregory W. Meeks, NY
X	Steve Chabot, OH		Albio Sires, NJ
	Joe Wilson, SC	X	Gerald E. Connolly, VA
	Michael T. McCaul, TX		Theodore E. Deutch, FL
X	Ted Poe, TX		Brian Higgins, NY
	Matt Salmon, AZ		Karen Bass, CA
X	Tom Marino, PA		William Keating, MA
X	Jeff Duncan, SC	X	David Cicilline, RI
X	Adam Kinzinger, IL	X	Alan Grayson, FL
X	Mo Brooks, AL	X	Juan Vargas, CA
X	Tom Cotton, AR		Bradley S. Schneider, IL
	Paul Cook, CA		Joseph P. Kennedy III, MA
X	George Holding, NC		Ami Bera, CA
	Randy K. Weber, Sr., TX	X	Alan S. Lowenthal, CA
	Scott Perry, PA	X	Grace Meng, NY
X	Steve Stockman, TX	X	Lois Frankel, FL
	Ron DeSantis, FL	X	Tulsi Gabbard, HI
X	Doug Collins, GA	X	Joaquin Castro, TX
X	Mark Meadows, NC		
X	Ted S. Yoho, FL		
X	Luke Messer, IN		

2/27/14 Foreign Affairs Committee Markup Summary

The Chair called up H.R. 2548 for consideration by the Committee.

H.R. 2548 (Royce), "Electrify Africa Act of 2014."

1. By unanimous consent, Royce-Engel 73 (an amendment in the nature of a substitute previously provided to Members of the Committee) was considered the base text;

    a. Rep. Meadows offered an amendment, Meadows 29, agreed to by voice vote.

H.R. 2548, as amended, was agreed to by voice vote, and ordered favorably reported to the House by unanimous consent.

The Committee adjourned.

www.ingramcontent.com/pod-product-compliance
Lightning Source LLC
Chambersburg PA
CBHW080440290526
45791CB00008BA/2560